Kindle Fire HD

Owner's Manual

Discover the Secrets of Your Tablet

Copyright

Summary

The Amazon Kindle Fire HD is one of the most unique digital readers on the market. It can do more than just display books, newspapers and magazines while you are on the go. It can also get you online and play back all sorts of media files. In fact, the things that you can do with it go well beyond what you might expect to get out of a traditional digital reader.

Using the Amazon Kindle Fire HD is a brand new guide that offers information on everything you've ever wanted to know about this unique reader. It is an easy to read and understand guide that offers step by step information on the many things that can be done with it.

This guide offers a number of sections about how you can use the online network to get access to all sorts of things for your Kindle Fire HD. You'll learn about not only how to buy things through it but also how you can get access to some free stuff. These include free books, free applications and many other items.

You'll also learn how you can download and install things onto your Kindle. The process of downloading and installing items directly onto it will not be all that hard to handle. In fact, you will even learn how to root your Kindle so you can get third party applications that aren't available through the Kindle store onto your reader.

There are individual sections in this guide dedicated to the many different kinds of programs and functions that can be supported by the device. These include sections involving how to play back music and video files, how to read a book on the device and even how to use different applications. There's even a section about how you can get your home videos and pictures uploaded to your reader.

You will also learn how to handle every single control on the Amazon Kindle Fire HD. The controls that you can use are made to not only adjust the visibility of your reader but to also get online. You'll learn how to connect to a Wi-Fi network, how to set up a payment account and even how you can turn the cloud off for privacy purposes.

The guide features plenty of photos relating to everything that you can do with the Kindle Fire HD. These photos show you information on what you will expect to see on your Kindle as well as what you might see with different apps and third party programs that you'll need to use when handling your Kindle. There are also plenty of pictures of what you will be getting yourself into when you are setting up your Kindle Fire HD on the Amazon website.

You should definitely see what this special guide has to offer when it comes to learning about what you can get out of the Amazon Kindle Fire HD. The things that you can learn from this guide will help you out with understanding not only what you can do with this reader but also how you can use this reader.

Introduction

The original Amazon Kindle was a revelation when it came out in 2007. The Kindle made it easier for people to read books while on the go. It was like bringing an entire library or bookshelf along with just one simple tablet.

Since then, the world of digital readers has substantially evolved. Today's portable readers are capable of performing the same functions that tablet computers can use. The Amazon Kindle Fire HD is one such reader that can do more than just display books.

You can use the Kindle Fire HD for all sorts of great online activities. It can be used with a web browser that links to a Wi-Fi network and even operates with support from Amazon's cloud.

You can also play back audio and video files on the Kindle Fire HD. It's also easy to buy and stream new movies or music when you connect the Kindle to a Wi-Fi network. Office documents and presentations can be displayed on your Kindle too.

The world of programs that you can experience with this reader is especially vast. You can download a variety of different applications ranging from productivity apps to portable games. There are even some apps that can help you protect your kids as they use your reader.

As you will see in this handy guide, it is very easy to use the Kindle Fire HD. It up only takes a few steps for you to get it all set up. The settings menus are also easy to move around and control.

Shopping for new content is also a breeze on the Kindle Fire HD. You can even pay for items with just one click without having to enter in your payment information every single time you want to get something.

Take a look at this guide and you'll see just how exciting the Kindle Fire HD truly can be.

Table of Contents

Part 1 – Fast Start

Why a Kindle HD?

You should first think about how a Kindle Fire HD has many differences that make it special and unique when compared to a Kindle Fire 3G:

1.   The Kindle Fire HD has a 1280x800 screen with support for 720p signals. The 3G only uses a 1024x600 screen.
2.   The HD uses Dolby Audio speakers while the 3G only uses stereo speakers.
3.   The HD can handle 16 or 32 GB of data depending on the model. The 3G works with 8 GB.
4.   The interface on the HD uses support for ten points on the multi-touch feature versus two for the 3G model.

The advantages of the Kindle Fire HD especially make it useful:

1.   It lets you browse the web with a cloud-supported browser.
2.   It uses a battery that lets you handle it for more than ten hours at a time.
3.   You can store your content on the Amazon cloud for free.
4.   The 7-inch screen is very easy to adjust in terms of brightness.
5.   You can use many different connectors for different items. These include HDMi and mini-USB connectors.

Firing Up the Kindle

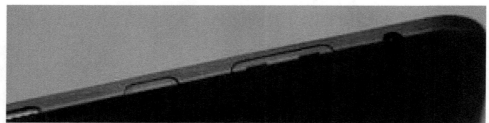

From left – power button, volume controls, headphone jack

The process of starting up your Kindle Fire HD for the first time is easy to understand. Here's a look at what you have to do in order to get your Kindle up and running.

First, you have to turn the device on. You can do this by using the simple button located at the side of the device. This should be next to the headphone jack and the volume buttons.

Navigating the Screen

It is very easy for you to navigate your way around the Kindle's touchscreen. There are a few things to be aware of:

1.   The screen is arranged initially to come with a standard book layout. This will have a vertical appearance to it. You can always use a horizontal landscape display too.
2.   The speakers should be on the top part of the device. These speakers will feature a small series of holes.

3. The HDMI plug and micro-USB port are both on the bottom when viewing in landscape mode.

4. The power button, volume controls and headphone jack should be at the right side while in landscape mode.

Registering

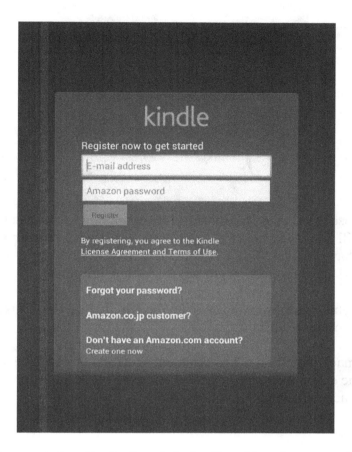

Registering your device is easy to handle. In fact, it is the first thing that you will be asked to do when you start up your Kindle Fire HD for the first time. Here are a few steps:

1. Turn on your Kindle Fire HD. The screen that you see above this listing should be the first thing that you see when you turn it on for the very first time.

2. Connect your Kindle Fire HD to a Wi-Fi network.

3. Choose the time zone that your Kindle is to work on.

4. Register your Kindle by either creating a new Amazon.com account or by using your existing account.

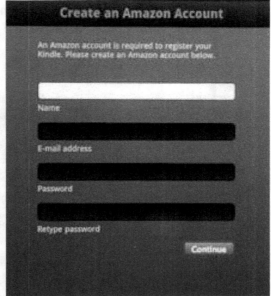

5.   You will have to use the Create an Amazon Account option in the event that you do not have an Amazon account. This will allow you to get your Amazon account set up with your name, email address and a password that you have created. You will type in the password twice as a means of confirming it.

6.   You finally have to agree to the terms of use for getting it running.

You can then get your payment information set up on the Kindle Fire HD. This can help you to pay for the items that you buy off of the reader.

The payment process is made with the 1-Click Payment Method in mind. This is used to allow you to pay for items by using one single touch of the screen while on the Kindle store. You need to use these steps in order to get your account set up:

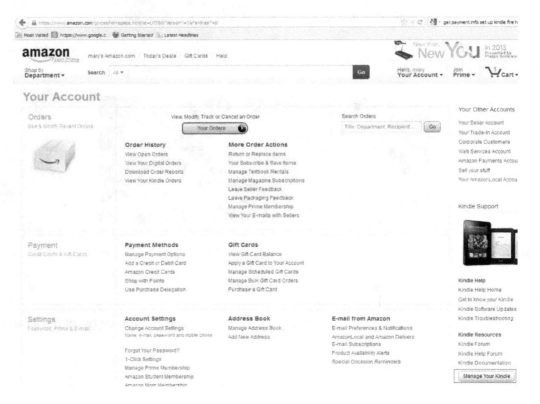

1.   Log into your Amazon account from a computer.
2.   Go to the Your Account section.
3.   Click on the Manage Your Kindle section.

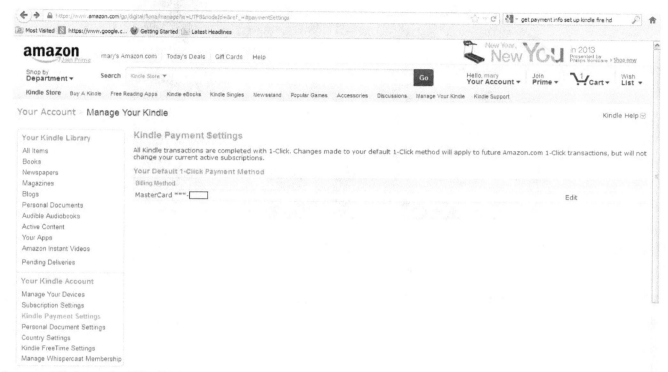

4.   Click on the Kindle Payment Settings section.
5.   Enter in the information relating to what you want to use to pay for items.

You can also choose to deregister the Kindle later on by going to the Settings and choosing the deregistration option. This will allow you to remove your identity from the Kindle and will allow another person to use the Kindle with one's own account.

Battery Charging

You will have to charge the battery on your Kindle Fire HD in order to get it to work. You can do this by simply using the battery charger that comes with your device. It will connect to the bottom of the reader.

The USB charger is the basic charger that you can use. You may also use a wall charger (see above) but that is sold separately.

It takes about four hours to fully charge the battery on a wall outlet and longer if you connect it to a USB drive.

You can tell that your battery is charging by taking a look at the power button. It should be lighting up as it is charging.

Navigating the Carousel Interface

The Carousel interface is the key interface that you will see when you start up your Kindle. You can navigate through this by waving your finger along the sides of the icons to access what you have.

This will show you the most recent applications or documents that you have opened. You simply need to touch the appropriate icon to get access to whatever it is you are looking to open up.

Finding Libraries

You can find your items in the many libraries listed in the device. You can use the Kindle to look up items in all sorts of libraries including ones for your books, videos, music files and applications. You should be able to access them by touching the appropriate link at the top of the Carousel display. You can work with one of these different libraries:

1.   Book library; it lists your books by title or author
2.   Music library; it can arrange items by artist, song title and album
3.   Video library; this can work for movies and television shows
4.   Documents library
5.   Apps library showing you all your downloaded applications
6.   A web link used to get you online

Free As a Bird

The key benefit of getting these libraries is that there is no need to lug all sorts of books around. This makes it easier for you to take whatever you want anywhere you go. You really are free as a bird when it comes down to it.

Clearing Your Browser History

You can clear the data on your browser by using these steps:

1. Tap the Web section.
2. Go to the Menu and then Settings
3. Go to the bottom of the section to clear your cookie data, history and cache.

Designating Favorites

You can also state your favorites among different items that you have on your Kindle for easy access to them. Here's how you can designate an item in the Carousel as a favorite:

1. Hold the item in your Carousel with your finger.
2. Select Add to Favorites when the prompt appears.
3. You can do the same again when you want to remove it from your favorites.

What on Earth is Whispernet?

Whispernet is the official Wi-Fi network that Amazon uses for Kindle products. It lets you get online for free with no subscription required. Fees for the delivery of some kinds of content may apply.

Status Bar and Option Bar

The top of the Kindle should list the status of the device. This includes listing information on who owns the Kindle, the time of day, the connection you have and the battery power left.

The option bar will open up when you tap the top area near the status bar. There are several things that are included in this bar. These items are the following:

1. The ability to lock or unlock the device
2. A volume control
3. A brightness control
4. A wireless networking menu that lets you turn networking on or off; this can include choosing an appropriate network
5. Sync feature to sync your reader to a larger device
6. The More button; this leads you to info on your account, parental controls and more

---

Urgent Business Opportunities in Nigeria

Be aware of what you are getting out of your Kindle. There is always the potential of spam coming in the way of your device at any time.

Using a Mini-USB Connector

The HDMI outlet and mini-USB connector. These are on the side of the Kindle.

You can transfer content from a computer to your Kindle Fire HD with a mini-USB connector:

1. Plug a mini-USB connector into the area near the power button.
2. Use the appropriate link at the other end of the USB connector to link up to the device.
3. The device should come up as a new storage device to add items onto.

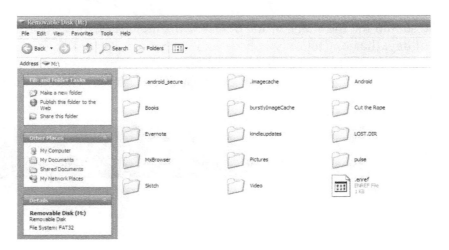

Rooting the Kindle

You could root the Kindle Fire HD if desired. Rooting involves altering the software to make it so you can get full control over what you want to do. It removes the limits that have been set up by the company that makes the product. This is useful **but it is recommended only for those with a great deal of experience in using the device.**

You can use a tool called Bin4ry Root Tool from http://uploaded.net/file/h44f6vni. Here's how to use it:

1. Download the program from the URL just listed.
2. Extract the download into a folder on your computer.
3. Open the Settings on your Kindle Fire.
4. Go to the Security section and enable the ADB.
5. Connect the reader to your PC with a USB plug after the drivers are installed.
6. Open the folder that you extracted the files into.
7. Open the RunMe file and press 2 and enter and then go to Special.
8. Press 1 and enter to go with the root option.
9. Follow the remaining instructions and the rooting process should be complete.

How to Tell Your Software Version

You can tell your software version by:

1. Go to More on the settings bar.
2. Go to the Device section.
3. Check on the System Version. This should tell you what version you have. It can be used to see if you have updated to the newest version of the software.

Can You Expand Memory?

Unfortunately, the Kindle Fire HD does not have support for external memory cards. You have to work with the 16 or 32 GB hard drive.

Fortunately, you can always get items off of your hard drive and onto the cloud when you wish.

Part 2 – Settings

This is the basic settings bar that you will see at the top of your Kindle when you tap the top of the screen. You'll need to refer to this area a number of times in this guide.

Guide to Quick Settings

The settings to use in the Kindle Fire HD are easy to understand. Here's what you will be using:

Unlocked – This will allow you to unlock the Kindle Fire so it can be freely used.
Volume – You can use this to adjust the volume as needed.
Brightness – This changes how bright the backlit display will be.
Wireless – Choose this to control the Wi-Fi network you are on.
Sync – Use this to sync your reader up to another device.
More – This will allow you to get into an additional menu that lets you adjust things like parental controls, the date and time and the keyboard.

Viewing Your Amazon Account on the Kindle

You can get access to your Amazon account through the reader. Here's how to do it:

1. Go to the More icon on the Quick Settings bar.
2. Touch the My Account bar.
3. This will show you the address that is linked to the Kindle.
4. You can touch the Deregister menu to remove the name from the account and to get a new account listed on the reader.

How to Control Sounds

To control sounds you can do one of two things:

1. Touch the Volume control.
2. Move the circle from left to right. Right means louder, left means quieter.

You can also choose to adjust the volume with the buttons on the side of the Kindle. The up and down buttons are used to adjust the volume to make it louder or quieter.

Adjusting Fonts, Typeface and Other Settings

You can adjust other things on your device with ease:

You can only adjust the font size on a book or on the eyeglass feature on the Silk browser. This can be adjusted by touching the "Aa" icon and choosing the proper font, margins, color and line spacing on the device. You can even get the Text-to-Speech feature turned off if you wish to use it.

Brightness

The brightness is adjusted by:

1. Go to the Brightness section of Quick Settings.

2.   Move the circle left to right to determine if you want a bright or dark screen.

Setting Up and Connecting with Wi-Fi

The Wi-Fi connection on your Kindle Fire is easy to handle. **It lets you connect online anywhere when a Wi-Fi network is available**:

1.   Go to the Wi-Fi section of the Kindle.
2.   Select On for wireless networking.
3.   Choose the appropriate network that you want the Kindle to connect to. In some cases you will have to enter in a password to get into a private Wi-Fi network.
4.   You can turn the Wi-Fi offer to using the Off switch.

Public Wi-Fi can also be used on your reader. You just have to activate the Wi-Fi in a space and then let it search for different Wi-Fi servers. You can tell that a public server is available based on whether or not there is a padlock attached to the signals on the left hand side of the entry. The fact that many public spots list their company or location names helps you to find them as well.

Syncing

The Sync feature is made to allow you to sync the Kindle with other devices. This can be done to get all the items you have in your Amazon account loaded to your Kindle.

The key is to make sure that the Whispersync synchronization feature is on. You can access this in the **Manage Your Devices** section of your Kindle account at amazon.com/manageyourkindle.

Using the Keyboard and Its Layouts

The keyboard is used to allow you to enter data in as needed. You can access the keyboard by simply selecting an entry point where you can enter data in. A keyboard should automatically appear.

The keyboard is made to work with a simple arrangement. It is used with a few important keys:

1.   The up key is used to get everything to be typed out in a caps lock format.
2.   The .com key simply adds .com to the entry. This makes entering in web addresses easier to handle.
3.   The keyboard icon with the down arrow will allow you to lower the keyboard.

There are a few different layouts that work on the keyboard. These can be accessed through the "123!?" button:

1.   The basic layout as seen above
2.   A layout that reveals the numbers, shift-based keys (@, #, $, %, etc.) and punctuation marks (?, !, :, ", etc.)
3.   Press the "+=" key on the second layout to reveal more special keys including math signs and even some specials like £, ©, ™ and ®

Changing the Background

You can adjust the background on your Kindle by using a few simple tips:

1.   Take a photo you have and resize it on your computer.
2.   Upload your photo to the Kindle. Refer to the appropriate section for moving pictures to the Kindle for details.
3.   Download an appropriate wallpaper app for the Kindle. This should be free to get in most cases.
4.   Add the photo on the Kindle to that app.

Set Up Notifications

Here's how you can control notifications:

1.   Check the More section.
2.   Go to the Applications file.
3.   Change the notifications by going to Notification Settings and choosing which ones you want to set on or off.

Settings for Travelers

You have to be aware of the settings that can change when traveling. Here are a few things to consider:

1.   You will need to use Airplane Mode if you are to use your device while on a plane. You can do this by going to the Wireless menu and choosing to turn off Airplane mode.
2.   You can check networks by allowing the Wi-Fi power to be turned on as needed.
3.   You may also touch the power button to put the device on standby mode when needed while traveling. This can conserve battery space.
4.   A separate AC power converter may be needed when going overseas. You can buy a converter separately.

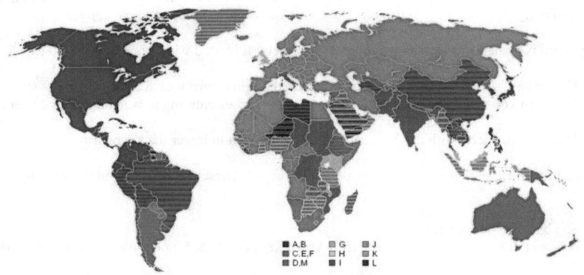

Which outlet will you plug your Kindle Fire HD into?

Part 3 – Shopping for Content

It's easy to go shopping for content on the Kindle Fire HD. You can buy new stuff for your Kindle through any section on the top of the screen.

Searching for Content on the Newsstand

The Newsstand is a part of the Kindle that allows you to find periodicals. Here's how to use it:

1.   Go to the Newsstand part of the front page on your Kindle.
2.   Click on the Store section on the top right corner.
3.   Select the appropriate section you want to use. You can search through magazines or newspapers.

4.   You then need to choose the right publication you want.

5.   You can finally choose to either subscribe to the publication for a certain period of time or choose to buy a single issue.

The most exciting thing about this is that you can find content in this section at values that are lower than what you'd expect on the shelf. You can save fifty percent or more on different items.

Browsing and Buying Books

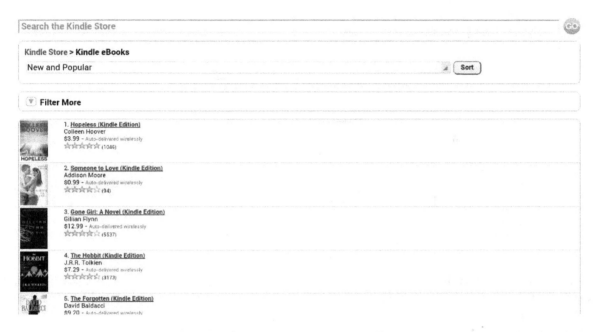

The process of getting books is especially easy to handle:

1.   Go to the Books section of the front page.

2.   Click on the Store link at the top right corner.

3.   You can choose to either search for items on the screen or search for a specific title or author through the search engine at the top.

4.   When you select a book you can choose to read a part of you. By clicking on "Try a Sample" you can take a look at a few pages of something for free.

5.   You can finally choose to buy the book by touching the yellow button that says "Buy for (price). The price will vary according to what a publisher has set but it may end up being less than what the original list price might be.

Kindle Buffet: Free Books, All You Can Eat!

An interesting part of getting books on the Kindle Fire HD is that you can find a number of books for free. This can work by simply taking a look at different places online:

1.   You can start by going to the Kindle Store on your Kindle Fire HD to find books in the public domain. Anything that was published prior to 1923 should be free to download.

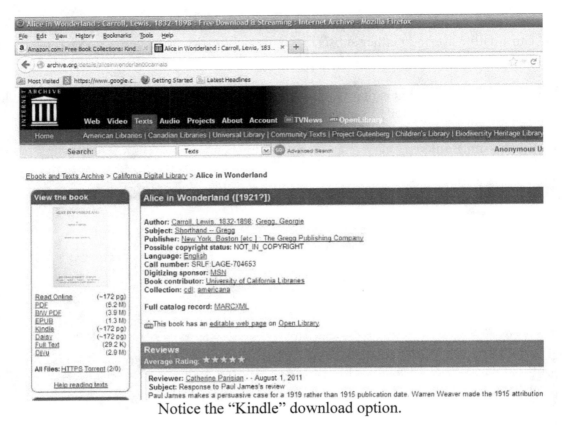

Notice the "Kindle" download option.

2.   You may also go to the Internet Archive website at archive.org. You just have to click on the Texts section of the site and then search through the right sections. You can download a .mobi file format that can be read on the Kindle and then upload that file to your PC.

3.   You can visit OpenLibrary.org to find old books as well. OpenLibrary.org will allow you to send files to your reader.

4.   Project Gutenberg at ProjectGutenberg.org can also provide you with free books that you can load up onto your reader.

Deleting Books

The process of deleting books is also easy to see:

1.   Go to the Books section.
2.   Touch and hold onto the cover of the selected book.
3.   Select the Remove from Device option.

Browsing and Buying Music

You can get music on your Kindle Fire HD as well. Here's a look at how to do this.

1.   Go to the Music section on the front.
2.   Click on the Store link.
3.   Search through the different items on the screen. You can search by genre, by bestseller, by new release or even by searching for a keyword at the top of the screen.

4.   Tap on an entry in order to open the item.
5.   You can choose to either buy the entire album or just buy individual tracks. It usually costs about a dollar per track or at least five dollars for a full album.

Browsing and Buying Video

The next part of shopping involves getting video files. Here's a look at what you can do here:

1.   Go to the Video section on the reader.
2.   Click on the Store link.
3.   There are separate sections for movies and television shows. Click on the one you'd prefer to use.
4.   You can choose to either rent a movie for twenty-four hours or buy the movie outright. It costs more to buy the movie permanently.
5.   You can also choose to buy television show episodes by the season or by the individual episode.

Note: You can get access to unlimited streams of all sorts of movies and television shows if you are an Amazon Prime member. You can get access to these videos at the top of the Video section of the store. However, it does cost extra to get this. You can learn more about this through the Amazon website.

Two Ways of Buying Streaming Video

You can choose to buy streaming video files by putting the purchases to your account. You can also use a gift card to give you credit to your device. This credit will work automatically if you upload an appropriate gift card code to your account. You may be able to find gift cards online or through different retail stores. It might work better for you if you want to keep from having to deal with credit card charges later on in time.

Searching for and Downloading Apps

It's also easy to get and download apps off of the Kindle's store:

1.   Go to the Apps section.
2.   Touch the Store link.
3.   Search for items based on your interest. You can search through the top margin or search based on category of interest.
4.   Choose a particular app of interest by touching on its icon.
5.   You can download it after you touch the appropriate yellow button. Some apps cost money but others are available for free.

Know Your Android

The process of getting downloads handled is similar to what you'd get on an Android device. However, you have to use the Amazon Kindle HD format to get files read. The file format used on Google Play is slightly different.

Installing an App

The installation process will work automatically after you click on an appropriate link to download it. This is done to simplify the process of getting the program to work.

How Many Apps Can You Have?

There is no limit as to how many apps you can get. The key involves taking a look at the amount of data you have to work with. You will be able to use a 16 or 32 GB hard drive on this device. This should be more than enough to handle whatever it is you want to work with when getting the device to work for anything you want to use it for.

The total amount of apps to use will depend on what you've got. You might be able to get at least a hundred apps on your reader if you don't have any video or music files on your reader.

Removing Apps

You can remove apps from the Kindle Fire HD with these steps:

1.   Go to the Apps section.
2.   Click on the Device marker at the top.
3.   Press the icon you want and hold onto it.
4.   Touch the Remove from Device message.

This will delete the app but it won't go away altogether. As you will see in this next part, you can permanently delete an app from your account altogether if you wish to do it.

Permanently Delete an App

The app you deleted will still be in the cloud but you can permanently delete it as well so it will not be on your account or your cloud data. Be aware that you will have to buy it again if you want it back:

1.   Log into your Amazon Kindle account through a computer.
2.   Go to the Your Apps section of your account.
3.   Choose an app and click on the Delete This App section of the Actions menu.
4.   This will end up removing your app altogether.

In-App Items

There are times where you might be able to buy new items within apps. The item that you can buy can vary by application but you should be aware of the three main types of in-app items you can get:

1.   Single device items are made to only work on the device you got it from.
2.   Multi-device items can work on any device that you can access an account for an app with.
3.   Subscription items can be automatically sent to your Kindle.

Transferring Items From an Old Kindle to New

You should get your old Kindle Fire items to move to a new Kindle Fire HD by simply using your cloud account. You can use the Whispernet cloud to get your items around if your old items are in the cloud.

You can also get your old Kindle's documents transferred onto a computer that you can attach the new Kindle Fire HD to.

Part 4 – Surfing the Web

You can use your Kindle Fire HD to work online in any place where you can get an appropriate Wi-Fi signal going. You just have to use a few simple steps for doing so. A key part of this involves the use of the Silk browser.

Silk is the official web browser that Amazon uses for the Kindle Fire HD. This is a unique browser in that it uses split architecture to make it easier to handle. Part of the power used for operating its functions will be on the Amazon server while the other part is used on your reader and the connection that you are using. It is done to make this work as quickly as possible.

A typical shot of what you'll see in the Silk browser.

Navigating the Web

You can use your tablet to move around different places with ease. You will be able to do this with a few steps:

1.	Open the Silk browser.
2.	You should be directed to a series of small links. This can feature a series of preferred links or even a history of the most visited spots that you have been to with your reader.
3.	You can choose to either touch one of these links or enter in another URL.
4.	Tap the top part of the browser to open up a keyboard. This will allow you to enter in any URL you want. You could also scroll all the way up to the top of the screen if you prefer.
5.	Touch the GO button when you have found the URL that you want to visit.
6.	You can then navigate the page by swiping different parts of the screen to move up or down or even from one side to the next. You can also tap different spots to select links that you want to go to.
7.	You can go back to the previous page you were on by touching the backward arrow at the bottom of your screen.
8.	You can also click on the plus sign at the top of the browser to open a new tab. You can click on any tab on your screen to move from one website to another. You will be using these two sites at the same time.

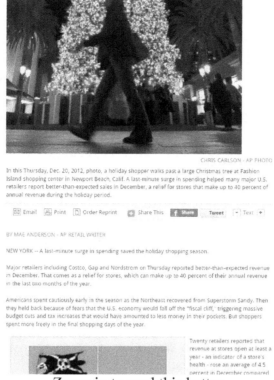

CHRIS CARLSON - AP PHOTO

In this Thursday, Dec. 20, 2012, photo, a holiday shopper walks past a large Christmas tree at Fashion Island shopping center in Newport Beach, Calif. A last-minute surge in spending helped many major U.S. retailers report better-than-expected sales in December, a relief for stores that make up to 40 percent of annual revenue during the holiday period.

Email   Print   Order Reprint   Share This   Share   Tweet   Text

BY MAE ANDERSON - AP RETAIL WRITER

NEW YORK -- A last-minute surge in spending saved the holiday shopping season.

Major retailers including Costco, Gap and Nordstrom on Thursday reported better-than-expected revenue in December. That comes as a relief for stores, which can make up to 40 percent of their annual revenue in the last two months of the year.

Americans spent cautiously early in the season as the Northeast recovered from Superstorm Sandy. Then they held back because of fears that the U.S. economy would fall off the "fiscal cliff," triggering massive budget cuts and tax increases that would have amounted to less money in their pockets. But shoppers spent more freely in the final shopping days of the year.

Twenty retailers reported that revenue at stores open at least a year - an indicator of a store's health - rose an average of 4.5 percent in December compared

Zoom in to read this better.

Zooming In and Out

The process of zooming in and out of a page is easy to handle:

To zoom in – Touch your fingers together at one point of the screen and then move them apart with the fingers still on the screen.
To zoom out – Keep your fingers apart on the screen and then move them together while on the screen.
To go back to original view – Tap the screen twice.

Be aware though that not all websites are capable of supporting this feature.

From left: Home, go Back, Menu, Search, Add to Favorites

Reading View

Reading View is a used to allow you to adjust the item you see on a site into a version that looks similar to what you would get on a typical Kindle Fire HD book. This works on websites that have plenty of text. This can create something that may be easier for you to read and will even preserve a number of the images and links on a page.

You can use this by simply touching the glasses that appear on the bottom of the screen. You can also adjust the size of the letters by touching the Aa sign while in Reading View.

You can get out of Reading View by touching the X at the top left corner of the screen. This will send you back to the regular page.

Bookmarking Pages

Bookmarking a page so you can access it later is easy to handle:

1.   Touch the bookmark-shaped icon at the bottom of your screen. This will lead you to a page that shows all of your bookmarks.
2.   Touch the page on the top left corner.
3.   Enter in the name of the bookmark and the location as prompted. This information should be filled out for you based on where you are.
4.   Your bookmark will be added and will be moved into the right spot in accordance with the alphabetical order of all your links. Be sure to watch for the title you give your page so you can make sure that it doesn't go into the spot alphabetically.

Searching the Web or From the URL Bar

You can easily search for different things online by using the right search engine. You can enter in the search engine address that you want to get on.

You can also use the URL bar at the top of your screen. This can help you to find items because it is linked up with a search engine that you chose in your Settings menu. Here's how you can use this:

1.   Tap the URL bar to open up the keyboard.
2.   Enter in anything that you want. Let's use "Carolina Hurricanes" for this example.
3.   When you enter in the phrase you will see a number of different keywords. When you enter in "Carolina Hurricanes" you will receive a number of keywords relating to the professional hockey team and many things associated with it.
4.   You can think touch one of the entries you get on the page. You can tap "Carolina Hurricanes tickets" to get results on places you can go to in order to buy tickets to one of the team's games, for instance.
5.   The results that are drafted will come directly from the search engine of your choice. You should then be able to search around the search engine page like you would for any other search.

Browser Options and Settings

You can reach the settings menu by touching the file drawer-shaped icon on the bottom of the screen. This should be in between the forward and bookmark icons. You can then touch the Settings icon.

The settings and options you can access are as follows:

General

1.   You can choose to go with Google, Yahoo or Bing as your search engine of choice.
2.   You can also adjust the size of your text and the default zoom option.
3.   There's an option to adjust the page to where it can automatically fit if you want it to.
4.   Images can be loaded automatically but you can choose here to keep them from loading like so.

Saved Data

There are several things you can do in this section to control your safety. This will be covered in the next part of this chapter.

Behavior

1.   Security warnings can be displayed if there are issues with the security of a page.
2.   Flash, JavaScript and pop-up windows can be activated or turned off through this. You may also choose to take them in on demand with the Kindle asking you for your permission to open something first.
3.   Pages can also open up in the background if desired.

Advanced Settings

1.   Text encoding is used to get the Kindle to automatically display foreign characters. The Latin-1 setting is the default but the UTF-8 coding may work well.
2.   The display view of the Kindle can be adjusted with a desktop or mobile setting. This can be used to adjust whether you want to see the standard version of a site or its mobile version. Going with the automatic option is best because it determines the appropriate display for a site automatically.
3.   You can even choose to reset all your settings to their defaults.

Privacy Settings and Options

The Kindle Fire HD will save data on your tablet based on the sites that you use. This may be convenient but at the same time it can be seen by others who use your reader. Therefore, you need to control your experience as well as possible. Here are some things you can do in this case.

First, you can go to the Saved Data section of the Settings menu. You can remove old private data or adjust how your Kindle collects data in one of many ways:

1.   An option to accept cookies is available.
2.   All cookie data, cached content and navigation history points can be cleared.
3.   You can opt to let the Kindle remember any form data that you enter. This includes data relating to usernames and passwords on sites you often go to.
4.   There's also an option that lets you clear saved form data.
5.   Passwords that you enter into different sites can be saved if you click this option.
6.   Passwords can also be cleared.

Privacy and the Cloud

Encryption can be used in your communications between your reader and the Amazon cloud. This will encode the transmissions made between both sides so they will not be picked up by unauthorized sources.

You can handle this by going to the Advanced section of the Settings menu. This will encrypt any data going between your reader and the Silk servers. Be aware that this may cause the pages you load to come up slowly.

Be aware that Amazon does collect IP addresses and store them for thirty days on their servers. These IP addresses do not identify the person who actually gets access to something though.

Turning Off the Cloud

You can also turn off the cloud in your Kindle Fire HD. This will allow you to go online without worrying about the cloud taking in your data. Here are some steps for you to use:

1.   Go to the Settings page on your browser.
2.   Uncheck the box that reads "Accelerate Page Loading."

You should be off of the cloud at this point. Just make sure that you watch for how your reader runs. It will more than likely slow down as a result of your adjustment.

Viewing Email

The final part of going online involves taking a look at the email on your reader. This can work with its own special application.

1.   Touch the appropriate Email application logo on your Kindle Fire HD's screen.
2.   You can choose the appropriate email provider based on what you want to access. You can use Gmail, Yahoo, AOL or Hotmail accounts but you can also use the Other selection too.
3.   Enter in your email address and password.
4.   You should now be in your appropriate email account. You can now read your email and even write and send emails from it.

Be aware that this does not work with Microsoft Exchange. That is not supported by the Kindle Fire HD at this time.

Avoid Viruses

You need to watch out when you are online so you can avoid viruses. There are a few things to do in order to avoid these issues:

1.   Always be responsible when you are online. This includes only going to websites that you trust.
2.   Don't open attachments sent to you unless you can trust whoever is sending them.
3.   Use a good antivirus program on your tablet. There are many free apps for you to get including the McAfee Mobile Security, AVG AntiVirus and Avast! Mobile Security apps.

Using Chrome

You can also get the Google Chrome browser to work on your reader. However, it is not available in the store. Here's how you can get this installed onto the reader:

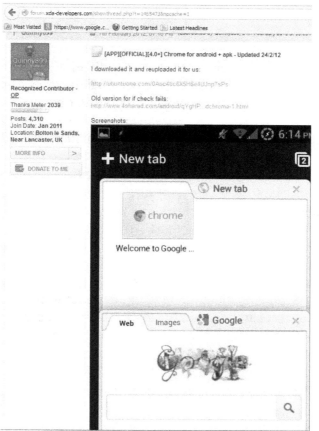

The view should be similar on your Kindle Fire HD.

1. Using your Kindle browser, go to http://forum.xda-developers.com/showthread.php?t=1485473.
2. Download the link on this site.
3. Let it install on your reader.
4. The app should be ready to use.

You can read books on the Kindle Fire HD with ease by handling the device with a series of useful controls. It is very easy to take advantage of this program and can involve a unique arrangement. In fact, you can do this with a variety of different documents in mind.

Personal Documents Service

The Personal Documents Service is a unique part of the Kindle Fire HD that makes it special. This feature is made with a system that helps you to handle personal documents of all sorts. You can read these documents on your reader without having to print anything out.

This can work with all sorts of different kinds of files. These include such files as:

Microsoft Word files   HTML files
RTF files   JPEG images
Kindle Format files including .mobi and.azw   GIF images
PDF documents   BMP images

Using Send-to-Kindle on Your Computer

You can also use the Send to Kindle application on your computer to move documents to your Kindle Fire HD. This program, which you can download from Amazon, will give you the choice to either right-click a document on your computer or send it as you are printing the item.

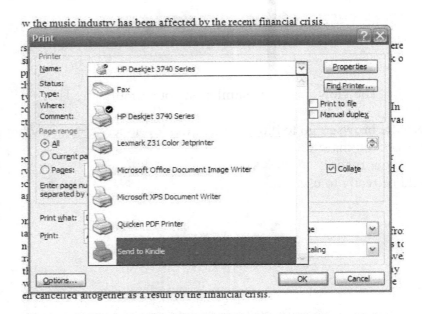

You can choose to send a document to Kindle from a print menu.

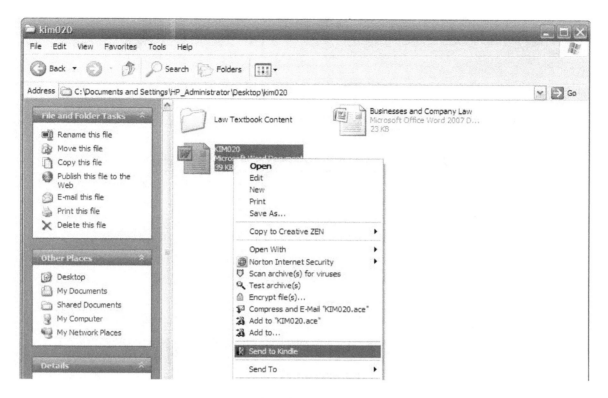

You can also right-click the item.

Keeping a Lid on @Kindle

Be sure that you keep your @Kindle data secure. The @Kindle system allows you to use a private account on your Kindle Fire. Just make sure that you keep all password information from anyone who wants to use your Kindle.

Converting Documents

You can convert documents on the Kindle Fire HD as well. You can do this with the Personal Documents Service.

1.   Go to your Amazon Kindle account on a computer's web browser and set up a Kindle email account if you do not have one. This will use the format (name)@kindle.com.
2.   Get the Send to Kindle program at amazon.com/sendtokindle.
3.   Install the program and then select a file you want to send to the Kindle.
4.   The file should be converted as it is being sent. It will be converted into a format that your Kindle can read.

Type Your Own Documents

You can also type your own documents on the Kindle Fire HD. The keyboard on the device makes it easy for you to type things and you can even use a stand to make it easier for you to type like how you would on a real computer (see the accessories section for details on a stand).

Welcome to Kingsoft Office

Dear user:

Thank you for using Kingsoft Office for Android. With its help, your life will be both easier and more efficient.

With the ability to edit documents on the go, you'll enjoy true office mobility.

With Kingsoft Office, you're able to view and edit documents locally or using cloud storage. The edit function includes text editing, format

Kingsoft in action.

However, it is best to get a separate application to help you out with typing these documents. The Kingsoft Office app is a good option to use. It is free to download on your Kindle.

Using the Book Library

The book library in your Kindle Fire HD is easy to handle. You can simply click on your book section and browse through your library's shelves. You can move your fingers up and down to go along different shelves and also search for books based on the author name, the title or what you have recently read.

Using the Kindle Owners' Lending Library

The Kindle Owners' Lending Library is a unique feature that allows you to borrow books from other people. **This is only for those who have paid extra to be Amazon Prime members**.

The steps for handling this are as follows:

1.   Go to the Books section of the store on your device.
2.   Go to the Kindle Owners' Lending Library.
3.   Touch the book entry that you want to get. You can also choose to search through the section to find books by keyword or author name.
4.   Touch the Borrow for Free icon.
5.   You can read the book with no due dates. However, you can only borrow one book at a time. Also, if you have one book borrowed during the calendar month then you will not be eligible to borrow another until the next calendar month. This is regardless of how long you borrow the book for.

Borrowing Kindle Books From a Library

You can even borrow Kindle books from your local library. The OverDrive service will allow you to do this. Here's how you can get books from a library:

1. Go to overdrive.com to see if a library in your area is able to handle the process in the first place.
2. Get a library card and a card PIN from the library you want to use.
3. Go to the website of the library of interest and look in the eBook section.
4. Choose the title you want.

5. Enter your library card information and then an email address to hold the book under.
6. Check out the book by adding to your cart.
7. Link your Kindle Fire to your computer through a USB drive.
8. The book should be loaded up to your device.

Navigating Books and Documents

You can use your Kindle to handle a book with ease. It's easy to navigate through the pages:

1.   To navigate forward you have to move your finger in a swiping motion from the right to the left. You will do the opposite when going backwards.
2.   You can get into different sections of the book by touching the appropriate highlighted spot in the table of contents.
3.   You can also touch the bottom of the screen to open up a listing stating what location you are on so you can fast forward to another section of the book.

Search by contents.

Searching Within Books

You can search within a book by touching the magnifying glass icon at the bottom of the screen. You should then enter in a word or phrase that you are looking for. You can then select the appropriate excerpt you want to find.

Bookmarking and Highlighting

To use a bookmark you have to touch the upper right hand corner of the screen. You can then access the bookmark on the Menu section. You can also remove the bookmark by touching the bookmark icon on the page you chose a second time.

Scyldings,
leader beloved, and long he ruled
in fame with all folk, since his father
had gone
away from the world, till awoke an
heir,
haughty Healfdene, who held through
life,
sage and sturdy, the Scyldings glad.
Then, one after one, there woke to
him,
to the chieftain of clansmen, children
four:
Heorogar, then Hrothgar, then Halga
brave;
and I heard that -- was --'s queen,
the Heathoscylfing's helpmate dear.
To Hrothgar was given such glory of
war,
such honor of combat, that all his kin
obeyed him gladly till great grew his
band
of youthful comrades. It came in his

Highlighting involves a different process. This can be done by doing the following:

1.   Touch the area you want to highlight for a few seconds.
2.   Drag your finger across the text to highlight.
3.   Select the Highlight option when it appears.
4.   The highlight can now be viewed in the Menu section along with your other notes. You can delete the highlight by holding your finger over that note and choosing the Delete option

Using the New American Oxford Dictionary

The Kindle Fire HD uses the new American Oxford Dictionary to help you find appropriate definitions of words when you need them. All you have to do is search for the appropriate item you want to look up and then the dictionary will look for it for you. Be aware that any entry that uses the word or words you search for will show up as you search for it. However, you can tell that the entry you want is listed when the word you searched for is the first thing to come up.

Part 6 – The Kindle Fire is Music to Your Ears

You can play music on your Kindle Fire HD with ease. Here's a look at what you can do.

Loading Music From Your Computer or the Cloud

Getting music from you computer to your Kindle Fire HD is easy to handle. You can do this via one of two options:

1.You can transfer your music onto you're the Kindle with a micro-USB connection.
2.You can transfer it from the Amazon Cloud.

The micro-USB connection works with these steps:

1. Make sure your Kindle is unlocked.
2. Drag the files you want to upload into the Music folder.
3. Eject and unplug the Kindle. The music should now be in your Music library.

The Cloud process works with this procedure:

1. Go to the music collection on your computer. iTunes is recommended in this case.
2. Upload the files in the music collection to the Amazon Cloud Player website at amazon.com/cloudplayer.
3. Your files should be accessible on the cloud.

Navigating Your Library

You can now navigate your Kindle Fire HD library via the Music section of the reader. Your data can be arranged based on the name of the artist, album or song.

You can read this information based on either the items on your cloud account or the items that are directly uploaded onto your device.

Searching for Music

You can easily search for much on your reader by doing one of two options:

1.   If you have music on the reader that you want to play you can use the magnifying glass tool at the bottom to search for music based on what you have.
2.   You can also go to the store section at the upper right corner to find new music to download.

Playing Songs

The songs that you play can be chosen by tapping the appropriate song or album that you want to play. The process of handling the music player is easy to understand:

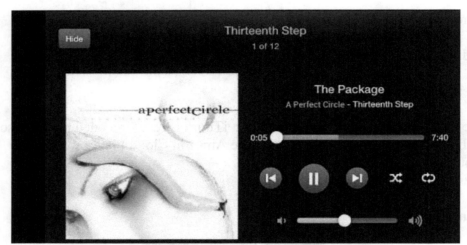

For the best results, use the landscape orientation.

Hide – Hide the player while it is playing music.
Song bar – The large circle shows where in the song the playback is located. The bold section shows what has loaded up if you are playing this from the cloud. You can adjust the position by holding and dragging the circle.
Back – Go back by one track.
Pause – Pause the music; you can touch again to resume playing.
Forward – Move forward by a track.
Shuffle – This lets you shuffle tracks.
Repeat – You can repeat this again after it is done playing.
Volume – Hold the circle to adjust the volume.

Internal and External Speakers

The Kindle Fire HD contains a series of internal speakers at the sides of the device. These are protected with a small metallic strip.

One of the internal speakers. Notice the metallic strip used for housing the speakers.

You can also use external speakers by plugging them into the headphone jack on your Kindle. This is provided that an appropriate 3.5mm jack is used on your external speakers to link the Kindle up to it.

Sound Quality

The sound quality on the device is particularly impressive. It works with the two internal speakers to help with differentiating between left and right sounds when headphones are not being used.

Creating and Editing Playlists

You can get a playlist set up by using a few steps:

1.   Go to the Playlists tab in your music library.
2.   Choose to Create a Playlist option and type in a name for your new playlist.
3.   Tap the + sign on the right side of each song to add it.
4.   Tap the Done button to finish it.
5.   You can tap the Edit button later on to edit this by dragging songs up and down, removing songs or using the same process used earlier to add new songs to the playlist.

Listening to Radio

You can listen to the radio on your Kindle Fire HD as well. There are many ways how you can do this:

1.   You can choose to go to an individual radio station's website and click on a streaming feature.
2.   You can also go to an appropriate application that you can download on your Kindle. The TuneIn Radio and iHeartRadio apps are the two most popular free options to get.

Part 7 – Video on the Kindle Fire

The Kindle Fire HD is able to play back video files with ease. It makes it easy for you to play a wide variety of videos including WMV, FLV, AVI, VOB, MVI, MPG, MOV, EVO and VP6 files among several other choices.

Controlling Videos

The volume control is at the top right.
You can pause the video on the bottom left side. You can also resume it from there.
You can control the position of the video on the bottom part.
A circle that reads "10s" can be used. This will allow you to rewind the video by ten seconds.

Streaming vs. Downloading

You can choose to stream or download video onto your Kindle Fire HD. There are many things to think about when it comes to these two options. Here are a few key comparisons:

1.   Streaming allows you to watch movies over a Wi-Fi network without having to download anything.
2.   Streaming can work well for any video size.
3.   Downloading does not involve having to worry about buffering midway through a video.
4.   Downloading does not require you to wait too long just to get a file loaded.

Streaming on YouTube and Other Sites

You can stream videos on YouTube and other websites with ease. This can include things like going onto the Amazon Prime site of the video store if you have a Prime account.

This will have the same playback arrangement as what you will have seen earlier. The key is that you will have to allow the video to load up over time and will need to be connected to an appropriate wireless network in order to get it to run.

Navigating the Video Library

You can navigate the video library on your Kindle Fire HD by moving around the Video section of the reader. Videos can be searched for based on the title or source and can be opened by simply tapping the video that you want to watch.

Where are My Home Videos?

You can get your home videos uploaded onto the Kindle Fire HD by using one of many options:

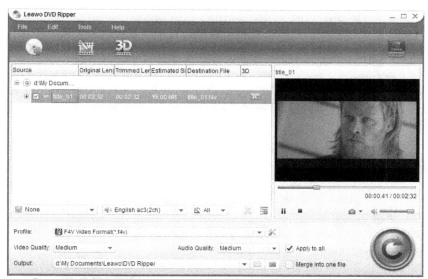

Leawo DVD Ripper, one of many programs you can use.

1.   One choice is to choose to upload a DVD to your Kindle Fire HD by using a special DVD to Kindle converter that is sold separately. You will have to load a DVD source onto a converter and then choose to upload the material to the Kindle. The Kindle has to be attached to the computer to get this to work.

2.   Another option is to take in any files that you have uploaded onto your computer and drag and drop them into the Video folder of your Kindle as it is attached to the computer.

Taking Your Own Pictures and Videos

The Kindle Fire HD also allows you to take pictures and videos as you see fit.

The front-facing camera on the Fire allows you to take pictures. This can even allow you to record movies with you on it. The steps are as follows:

1.   Go to the Apps section of the reader.

2.   Touch the Camera application.

3.   The controls on the application will let you take pictures with a single touch or even record video as desired. You may need to watch for what you are doing here because there is no rear camera on the reader.

Using Flash

Flash can be used for handling videos as well. However, Flash is automatically disabled by the Silk browser when you first use it. You can activate it by doing the following:

1.   Go to the Silk browser.
2.   Go to the Settings menu.
3.   Tap the Enable Flash section and select "Always On."

You can also get this ready by using the Dolphin browser. The browser should be installed this through the App Store on the Kindle. It will work with Adobe Flash automatically.

Download YouTube Video

It is easy to use YouTube on your reader like you could with any other streaming video site. You'll need to get an appropriate player set up though. The FREEdi YouTube Downloader is a good option to use. Here's how to get it:

1.   Go to the App store.
2.   Search for and download the free FREEdi YouTube Downloader.
3.   Open the device after you finish downloading and installing it. The installation should be done automatically after you download it.
4.   Choose an item on the screen or search for it by using the search tool at the bottom.
5.   Long press the item you want to download.

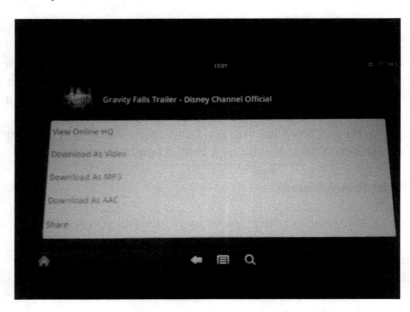

6.   You can then choose to download the file as a video or AAC file to use on your reader.
7.   Open the bottom menu and look for the Downloaded section.
8.   You can delete the video later by long-pressing the item and choosing the Delete option.

Part 8 – Viewing Home Video and Photos

You can easily view home video and photo files on your Kindle Fire HD. Here's a look at how you can transfer these photos to your device.

Transferring and Viewing Photos

Note: you have to make sure your Kindle Fire HD is unlocked in order to get this to work.

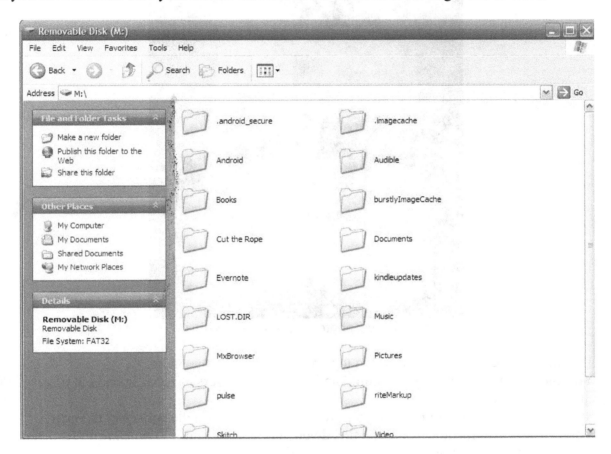

1.   Connect your Kindle Fire HD to your computer. Wait to see that your computer identifies the reader.
2.   Open the Kindle on the computer. It should look like a portable hard drive.
3.   Click on the appropriate picture file you want to move to the Pictures folder.
4.   Unhook the Kindle from the computer. You'll have to press the Disconnect button on the Kindle screen.

You should now go to the Gallery to view your photo:

1.   Go to the Apps section.
2.   Touch the Gallery icon.
3.   You can see your pictures by touching the appropriate thumbnail.

There are a number of tools to use here:

An awkward photo of a baseball uniform.

1.   The magnifying lenses can allow you to zoom in and out of the photo.
2.   You can also use a pinching or pulling motion on your fingers to zoom in and out of very specific parts of the photo.
3.   Swipe the screen with your fingers to move from one phone in the gallery to the next.
4.   You can access to menu to share the file, delete it or edit the video. You can edit its details, crop parts out or rotate it to the left or right.

Transferring Home Videos and Viewing Them

You can get old home videos transferred and loaded to your Kindle Fire HD with ease. Here's how you can do this:

1.   First, you have to transfer your old file onto your computer. This has to be done with a video transfer product that is sold separately if you have a traditional video cassette recording to work with.
2.   You then click on the appropriate file to move to your Kindle and drag it into the Video folder after connecting the Kindle to your computer (see above).
3.   You should then be able to access to video in your video folder.

Part 9 - Apps for Kindle Fire HD

You can use applications on the Kindle Fire HD in all sorts of forms. You can get Apps to work by going to the Apps menu of your device and by searching for what you have based on title, whether it's on the cloud or your device and even what you've recently opened. The process of using the Kindle for apps is very easy to handle.

In fact, opening your apps is easy to handle too. This can work by simply touching the icon on your app.

How to Get Free Apps

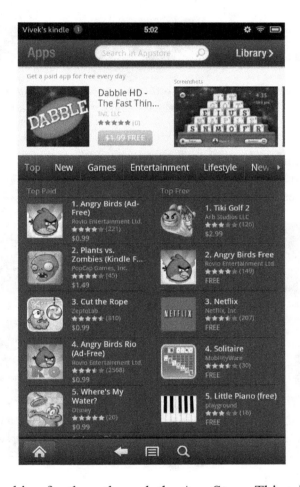

You can get free apps by searching for them through the App Store. This will allow you to look by checking on different applications for free. You can go to the Top Free section on the front page of the store. This is located at the right side of the screen.

Installing Third Party Apps

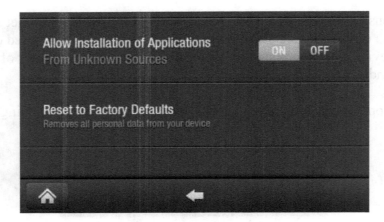

You can get third party apps uploaded onto your Kindle Fire as well. This is known as sideloading, a process where non-Android applications endorsed by Amazon can be loaded onto your reader.

1.   Go to the Settings section.
2.   Link to the More section.
3.   Tap the Device section.
4.   Allow unknown sources to install application.

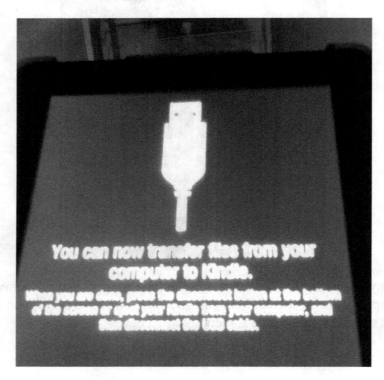

5.   Connect the Kindle to your computer.
6.   Download whatever software it is you want to add.

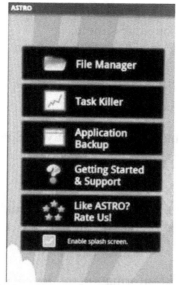

Astro, a popular file manager.

7.   Install an appropriate file manager program onto your Kindle.
8.   Copy the APK file that was downloaded to the device.
9.   Remove the Kindle from your computer.
10.   Open the file manager and find the directory that the APK is on.
11.   Tap the APK to install the program.

Must Have Apps

There will be a number of must-have apps that you need to take a look at so you can find something of use. These are some of the top must have apps that you need to take advantage of:

Netflix
This will allow you to stream movies and television shows from your tablet. This is provided that you have a paid Netflix account.

Pandora
This is used to allow you to listen to streaming music through a radio station programmed by your musical interests.

IMBd
The Internet Movie Database app lets you search for information on the tablet on all sorts of movies and the people involved in them.

The Weather Channel
You can get up to date weather information on what's happening in your local area through this app.

AndroZip Root File Manager
AndroZip allows you to organize and find files on your Kindle while also helping you to compress files as needed.

Drawing Pad
Drawing Pad creates a unique art tablet on your Kindle.

Flipboard
You can keep track of all your social networking feeds off of the Flipboard.

Dropbox
Dropbox is used to let you place files into an account that you can access on any Dropbox-supported device. You can download files from your account and add new ones to it as needed.

NewsHog
NewsHog lists a number of news channels from Google News and helps you to search through each individual channel for the latest information on whatever you want to learn more about.

ESPN ScoreCenter
This connects to the ESPN website to list information on the latest sports scores and news.

FreeTime

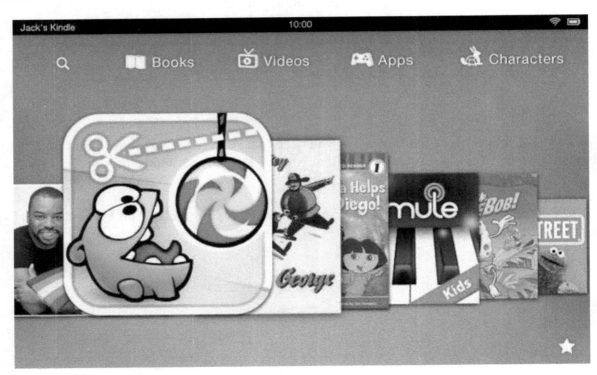

FreeTime might be one of the most valuable apps for you to use for your device. It is featured on the reader and will allow you to customize what your kids can experience when they use your reader. This includes allowing you to choose what items can be accessed and even limiting the amount of time that something can be used for.

This also allows your kids to view items in a nice interface with plenty of easy to use sections. In addition, your kids will not be able to access the web browser or store. Social networking is also disabled. This means that the tablet is not connected to any online material unless you activate the Wi-Fi signal via password.

The process for setting it up is easy to handle:

1.   Go to the FreeTime app.
2.   Set up a password. This can be the same as what you use for parental controls. You can also create and confirm your own password.
3.   Add a new profile for a child who will be using it.

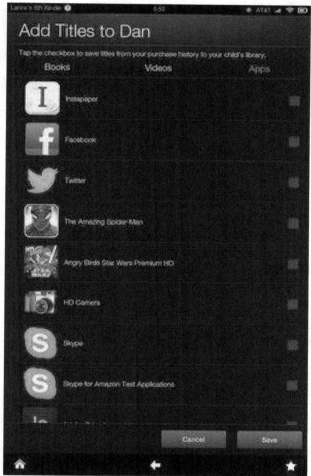
You don't want to let your child watch a PG-13 film, do you?

4.   Add the content that you want your child to be able to access.
5.   Touch the Exit button when you are finished saving the content. You'll have to enter the password again.

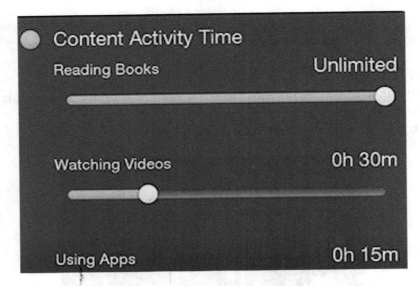

6.   Go to the More section of the screen to adjust the daily time limit that an account can handle.

Social Media Apps

It's already well-known that you can use the Kindle's browser to get access to social media sites. However, you can also get access to you social media accounts by using applications that help you get access to your accounts. There is also the option to set up these apps to automatically identify your account based on the login information you provide.

1.   The Facebook app that comes with the tablet allows you to long into your account with ease.
2.   A free Twitter app can also be downloaded.
3.   Pinterest has recently released a free app for the Kindle Fire HD.
4.   A third party application like Pocket Social may also be downloaded to help you out with linking up to multiple social networking sites.

PowerPoint Apps

You can particularly get a special app to help you watch PowerPoint presentations from your device. The Leawo PowerPoint to Kindle Converter help you convert files to a system that the Kindle can handle. Here's how you can do it:

1.   Download the app at http://www.leawo.com/powerpoint-video-converter/. You then need to install the appropriate program.

2.   Import the PowerPoint files you want to have converted to the program.

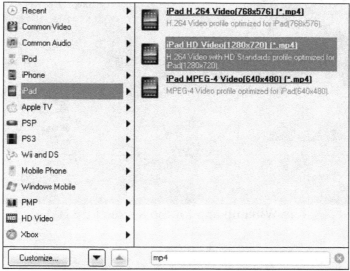

3.   Select the appropriate output format. An interesting point about the program is that you can use the .mp4 format even though it says "iPad HD Video." The format still works on the Fire HD.

4.   You may then customize the settings to include a different file name, a timing solution that allows the slides to be displayed for a specific period of time before moving on and so on.

5.   The files can then be converted.

6.   You should then drop and drag the finished files to the appropriate video section of your Kindle. This is provided that the Kindle is linked to your computer.

Getting a Media Player

You may choose to get a media player set up for your Kindle Fire HD as well. This can work if you want something other than your traditional media player on the device.

There are several free and paid media players for you to find at the app store. These include VPlayer, Winamp, Roku, Skifta and VLC Super Duper Remote among many others. The process of getting one is easy to handle in that you just download something and let it install on its own.

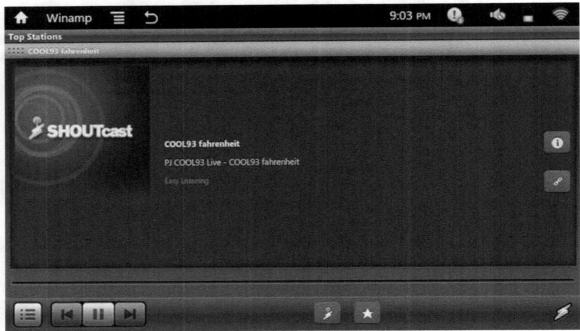

The Winamp app for the Kindle Fire HD.

Part 10 – Feed Your Kindle with Web Content

You can get new web content added to your Kindle Fire HD with ease. Here's a look at what you can get out of it.

Using Calibre with the eBook Reader

Calibre is a program that allows you to link convert online books into formats that your Kindle can read. You can use this with a few easy steps:

1. Download the Calibre program onto your computer at Calibre-ebook.com
2. Add any eBooks you have to the program.
3. Click on the books you want to convert and then go to the Convert Books button.
4. Set the books to the .mobi format.

5. Remove the [PODC] command from the Personal Doc Tag folder.
6. Click to convert the books.
7. Copy the book files to the Books folder on the reader.
8. The books should now be in the Books section of your reader.

This can work with all of the news that you want to handle. You can get different PDFs from news publications converted onto the program for free through Calibre. You won't have to pay anything extra outside of what you have gotten out of the subscription that you have used.

Let's Go Shopping!

You can go shopping to find different items of interest on the Kindle Fire HD. This can all work with your special site to make it easier for you to get something of use on your tablet.

The big thing about what you can get here is that the choices you have for downloading items can vary based on what you want to get. The choices you have are going to change over time.

Exploring Calibre Further

There are many other things that can be done on Calibre. You can do these things with the free program:

1.   You can add new font families into different books to make them easier to read.
2.   Graphics in eBooks are now easier to upload. This is especially the case for math equations.
3.   PDF support is made with full pagination support.
4.   The Fetch News icon can be used to help you get news off of the device from any feed that you want to use.

Kindlefeeder

Kindlefeeder is particularly useful for getting different feeds arranged into an eBook format. It works with a simple arrangement:

1.   Sign up for the service at kindlefeeder.com.
2.   Go to the Manage Your Kindle section of your account on the Amazon website and add kindlefeeder.com to your list of approved emails to get messages from.
3.   Choose the appropriate feeds that you want to get Kindlefeeder to load up on. You can do this with your account on kindlefeeder.com.
4.   Connect your Kindle to a Wi-Fi network to make it so your device can handle an appropriate downloading process to get your feeds downloaded.

This can work provided that you follow the rules. You can get up to twelve feeds and 500 KB of images for free. A premium membership of $20 a year will give you access to more feeds and up to 4 MB of images.

Part 11 – Accessories for Your Kindle Fire

The Basics

You'll need to get a number of accessories to use with your Kindle Fire HD. These include such things as the following:

1.   A USB connector to help get your Kindle to link up to a computer
2.   A portable travel charger; this can include something that can be plugged into a car's electrical outlet
3.   A wall charger to help you charge up the battery as needed
4.   A screen protector; this can include a small clear cover that works on your Kindle Fire to protect it from smears or scratches

Printer Link

You can get a printer link to work on your Kindle Fire as well. It is easy to use a Bluetooth adapter to link up to a printer that has Bluetooth support. This should allow you to get anything that you have printed with ease.

You'll need to get an appropriate printing app ready though. The EasyPrint app is a good choice to use.

Cases, Kickstands and Other Covers

You can get a case to work on your Kindle. This can be used to store your Kindle in while also being used to protect it from damages in the event that it is dropped. A case can particularly be used to cover up the Kindle to insulate it. You can even use a cover to add a little bit of a visual flair to it.

A good case can include a number of valuable items. These include the following:

1.   A kickstand can be used on your case. This will be used with a bending motion and a grip to help keep the reader upright while using it.
2.   Pockets can be used in your case as well. These can include pockets that go on the back or on the inside cover of the case. You can store small papers or items inside one of these pockets.

3.   Attachments can also work on cases. An attachment may include something like a keychain that goes on a loop around your Kindle.

Pouches, Envelopes and Sleeves

One of Amazon's many marketed pouches and sleeves.

Quality pouches, envelopes and sleeves can be used as items that you can store your Kindle in without risking it being damaged. These items are made with special materials used to insulate what you have. They can also feature fasteners or zippers to keep the inside of the pouch or envelope protected.

You do have to take the Kindle out of one of these materials in order to get it to work. However, this can prove to be useful when getting your Kindle protected.

Speakers and Headphones

Getting headphones attached to the Kindle Fire is very easy to handle. You can use a basic 3.5mm jack to get headphones into your device. This should work with just about anything you have to carry around.

Ear buds are particularly notable items to use for your needs. An ear bud is a type of material that fits directly into the ear so you can listen to items with it. This kind of headphone option is very small and can be easy to wear.

The MatchStick speaker dock is one example to use.

However, you might want to get speakers to work for your device. You can use these speakers in one of two ways:

1.   First, a speaker can be plugged into the headphone jack on the Kindle to get it to work.
2.   Second, you can insert the Kindle into an appropriate base. This may work with the micro-USB port. The example shown above is a good idea to take a look at.

Stylus

Styluses to use.

A stylus is a type of material used to allow you to write on the Kindle Fire HD's screen. It is used like a traditional pen but with a solid arrangement and a contoured tip. The device is used to help you out with touching the right spots on the Kindle so it will be easier for you to use for any purpose.

Stands

The last of the accessories to use is a good stand. This can be separate from a case but it could still make using the Kindle or displaying it easier to handle.

A stand can be arranged with an angle to allow the Kindle to be displayed. It will come with a small edge at the bottom to place the Kindle on. This kind of stand doesn't have any ports or connections but it is simply used to get the Kindle to be easy to place and use when on a desk or other flat surface.

One person even created his own stand. You can also buy a professionally made one if desired.

Conclusion

It's amazing to see just what you can do with your Amazon Kindle Fire HD. This reader is made to give you the ability to do more than what you might expect with a reader.

You can use the Kindle Fire HD to read books with ease. Your Kindle is made to help you not only display books but to also let you adjust the size of the text, bookmark passages of interest and even highlight spots that you want to refer back to.

It's also easy to get media files played back on your Kindle. You can even use a separate media player that you can download if you wish to go down that route with it.

Your Kindle is also made with a number of different controls made to give you the best possible experience with it. The keyboard control is easy to handle as is the touchscreen that you'll use for controlling your experience. Even the controls on the physical body of the Kindle are made to help you out with keeping it under control.

It's especially easy to get online with the Kindle Fire HD. The only things that you would have to pay for when you are online are the purchases that you actually make while you are on the Wi-Fi network. The Wi-Fi access on the Kindle is made to work in many spots and should not be all that hard for you to set up.

Don't forget to take a look at the accessories you could be using with your Kindle. Stands, chargers, stylus pens and speakers can all be added to make the Kindle more useful and entertaining.

Be sure to play around with your Amazon Kindle Fire HD and see what it has to offer. There truly is a vast world of things that you can do with this amazing device.